THE RED-HEADED PUPIL

T0124425

By the same author from Carcanet

Selected Poems

The Red-Headed Pupil

and other poems

JEFFREY WAINWRIGHT

CARCANET

Acknowledgements

'The Anatomy Lesson' appeared under the title 'The Red-Headed Pupil' in *PN Review* 80, July-August 1991.

An earlier version of 'The Weak Spot' appeared in *The Flying Pig*, Department of English and History, The Manchester Metropolitan University, Autumn 1991.

'Free Rein', no XXI, under the title of 'Cause and...' the *Independent* 3rd February 1994.

The Judith E. Wilson Fund, the Faculty of English and St John's College, University of Cambridge, for a Visiting Fellowship in Autumn 1985.

The Head of Department and colleagues in English and History at The Manchester Metropolitan University for sabbatical and personal support.

To Mike Fuller, Elspeth Graham, Avril Horner, Alf Louvre and Brian Maidment who have given me advice and encouragement at important times, and special thanks to Michael Schmidt and Judith Wainwright.

First published in 1994 by
Carcanet Press Limited
208-212 Corn Exchange Buildings
Manchester M4 3BQ

Copyright © 1994 Jeffrey Wainwright

The right of Jeffrey Wainwright to be identified
as the author of this work has been asserted
by him in accordance with the Copyright,
Designs and Patents Act of 1988.
All rights reserved.

A CIP catalogue record for this book
is available from the British Library.
ISBN 1 85754 086 7

The publisher acknowledges financial assistance
from the Arts Council of Great Britain

Set in 10 pt Galliard by Bryan Williamson, Frome
Printed and bound in England by SRP Ltd, Exeter

For Tom and Holly
minds of their own

'In vain sedate reflections we would make,
When half our knowledge we must snatch, not take.'

Pope, 'Moral Essays', Epistle I

Contents

The Red-Headed Pupil

Part One: The Anatomy Lesson

Prologue

Holly, how far you are from dying,
how far from ever dying! Such a head
of hair, a real bonfire flaming in the street,

happy in your skin, at least as much as
most of us could hope to be, well certainly
lucky-ish so far for nineteen years
with your trapped thumb your only lesion

or serious bump from life – admit it!
Look how the city concrete can turn rose
in the four o'clock winter sun –
Then don't – pick what you want for your mind,
things of your own to make the neurons fire!

I

In some river, any day of the week,
some figure bumps against the bridge-pile
and is left as the current passes.

One could be draped in with rags and branches,
another arched and stretched like a backstroker
starting, another sprawled on a settee,
perhaps slalom poles bob on their wires nearby.

Whoever comes there just turns up without
benefit of bread packed with mercury
and cast upon the waters: one who maybe
watched the weed-tresses combed by the stream, carried
an air-gun for rats, or just came and walked in.

II

For this bridge the firemen have a drill set.
Though the channel is wadeable to the bar,
then they are in the full, deep-cut race

so must be equipped up to spec, their skill
tallied to the job in hand so that a hoist
and a cradle-drop from the second span
can lean over and draw him from the flume.

To be re-gathered, re-numbered,
an obligation set by the hopeful
ordinance that none shall be lost in death,
that given names shall be found, and a duty done
each effaced, replaceable citizen.

III

Exact cause: something to be found, something
to be entered, a last dent that can stand
as this man's very last particular.

Imagine a wooden country room.
The township pathologist parts the skull,
perhaps handing the cap to his assistant
who holds it out like a small basin

as he unfolds the brain down either cheek,
teasing from the centre-parting of hemispheres
something that looks an impractical pink,
silly, more like an unravelled pullover
splashed with gloss and emulsion than hard-wiring.

IV

Is this where what the man is is to be found?
Is this where it all coincides, is all
gazetted, cartouched, ephemerized,

but in wisps and bobbles, not even in
circuits like the droplet solderings that sang
'*It might as well rain until September*',
'*He's a rebel and he'll never ever be any good*'?

The caretaker's small boy steals to the open door –
he wants to know what's up there but the feet
fill his view, blebbed, blistered, blained, the unique
dogs of infantry and chiropody –
'*Excused boots? What makes you so different?*'

V

Squeak. In a boarded nook only its own size
a mouse can hide and never pine for light,
but even so it cannot help but be.

Since everything true of a mouse and me,
as everything true of Thomas Nagel,
is already in the world – the world that is
just the world – how can we then be we

and not any of those who got off the bus
at the top of Duke Street one afternoon,
and disappeared until now, dipped deep
in the spoonable white medulla –
what is it like? How can they be them?

VI

Mad in the night with dreams ('human beings
by definition half the time mad' anyway?)
I am looking down on my own dissection.

Not Vesalius completing his book,
nor Doctor Tulp showing with his scissors' tip
how the tendons of the open forearm lie
and how the annular ligament

keeps all of them in place, could look on this
more disinterestedly than I myself –
certainly not the red-headed pupil
who looks perplexed as though the stripped-out arm
has already waved his mind elsewhere.

VII

My chest is sprung open, all abdominal
muscle and cartilage sheared away
and under the sternum where the heart

and the blue lungs lived is now a cave
a small cat could climb in. Down there, or up here,
one of us ought to be scared – squeamishness
arrives routinely at even the sight

of a punctured thumb and this must be the worst
that could ever happen. But none of it hurts,
no damage is done, it is just interesting.
We are free of each other and free:
just as we always thought, we do not die.

VIII

Mad in the night with dreams... Suitcases packed,
everything we own, including blankets,
crowding the bay of somebody's front-room,

and I see over the backs where I played
and the haulage-yard of still-wet
shiny Fodens, swans crossing the sky
over Normacot, and then, very low,

a stubby airliner, much like Richard Scarry
would draw and call 'Mirabelle',
hanging upside down tethered by cables
and rigging which people are fleeing down
while others fall on daisy blooms of parachutes.

IX

Some do escape, but then the crash is real.
It is down on Buccleuch or Furness Road
and I am caught too close to do nothing.

I pick up the suitcases – all those blankets –
and set off, showing myself how
properly eager I am, but with the hope
that I will walk and walk and be too late.

Yet nothing that comes to my eyes is,
after all, insupportable. All is earth,
muddied figures, plasticine men, obscure.
Beyond the tape the crater is too deep to see.
I carry my suitcases here then there.

X

Is that how the brain makes itself useful,
toiling while we sleep, like an engine-driver,
a nightwatchman with his box and brazier,

a fluffer gathering hair from the Tube rails,
evolving something else to be good at besides
the calculation of what's too hot or too heavy?
Must be a good part of what it's fit for.

Doctor Tulp, like the best of barbers, shoots
his cuffs and begins. He combs out the axons
and dendrites, the woven feltwork of us,
and touches – does he? – the man who husks and counts
onion-skins, then . . . a face like a pollard knot?

XI

Or are they, to Physics, the same kind of thing
as the soul, or a haircut? Observe what
we can; instance: the annular ligament.

Seven gather round Tulp to study it.
One is fixed on the master, 'Look, I'm listening',
the next looks knowingly at the book propped
by the corpse's feet, two are intent,

one relishing this, another checking his notes,
the sixth poses, the seventh is the red-headed pupil.
Close your fist. From their condyle, flexor muscles
travel the hairy side of the arm and cock
the wrist as well. We do that without thought.

XII

Because, said George B. Bridgman, the body is
a machine. For fifty years he drew it and taught
that the fixed law of muscle is to contract

towards its centre, and all the body's cords,
pulleys, levers, declutch accordingly.
So he strips the masseter to a hinge
that lets the head's one moving bone mill

its meal and oil; he draws as a trapeze
the muscle across the shoulders that keeps
the head erect; the back as hewn planes
and a fantail of cables wedged down
into the sacrum, the body's axis,

XIII

the free fulcrum on which it turns and flees.
The foot, he says, is the envy of bridge-builders:
its keystone astralagus is not fixed

as in masonry, but floats the weight
of the whole body between the heel
and the toes as it descends step by step
to the ground where it rocks, lifts and leaves.

And wherever two bones meet, the cartilage tip
takes up the jarr on a surface smooth as cellophane,
filmed by an oil, a tiny pressing of cells
'That supples, lubricates and keeps in play
The various movements of this nice machine.'

XIV

We do all of this without thought. Stop. All this
is done without thought. Because we are
a machine – because there *is* a machine,

like there *is* a wall abutting this street,
26 feet wide, a 1910, 3-
storey gable-end, 112 flights
though by now not one brick is the same shade and feel

as another. Thus, four-square as it is,
Halifax and Leeds permanent as it is,
without new downpipes or the way soot
has filtered outwards, it must be counted
but semi-invariant since every hour the light changes it.

XV

It is almost as particular as flesh,
and brick for brick, grain for grain, hair for hair
it is the same stuff, the same compo as us.

Examine one drop of water dried into the lime:
there is still a lake-bed upturned to view;
enter one fissure, abseil to its last
unsustainable point and new caverns fall open.

At this ground, whatever wattle the mind,
whatever surprise or animation,
whatever joke splutters and laughs to itself,
'this loam, this roughcast and this stone does show
that I am that same wall; the truth is so.'

XVI

'Would you desire lime and hair to speak better?'
No, but on some days to fade into it,
which I cannot do, *'O sweet and lovely wall'*.

We are after all too different.
Nobody walks into a wall, nor runs
through it – it *is* seen, even though, full on,
some of the bricks are known to be guessed at

from their neighbours as orange patched with grey –
again an extrapolation achieved
without thought. But it is up here, on the screen,
now, with some yellow flowers, more variant,
all information for area 17.

XVII

What do I sees here? *I* see nothing.
The machine works, the piece of work that bumps
against the bridge-pile works, and that is all.

I is the body's dream, what it makes up
as it goes along. The brain cranks I out
inadvertently as it feels thirsty
and puts the kettle on – one scope and a bit.

Forget homunculus, be he Happy,
Grumpy, Bashful, Dopey, Sleepy, Doc;
forget 'I spy', forget 'Up periscope!',
the earnest youth, the boy of feeling,
forget any soul behind the night-sight.

XVIII

In 17 the wall is projected sunny;
next door it is warm; a metal hanger
tings like a tuning fork. Sweet somatics,

how you develop to no purpose save
to be that bit better at it next time.
Individuals strive to increase
the representation of their genes

and that is all. Organisms adapt and
that is all. Matter is the ground: mind, God,
spirit, soul are words – lemony lichens –
workable static in the cellular
circuit boards, success[10].

XIX

Put a picture of the brain in your mind's eye.
Done? That's not the way it is. However
dispassionate you are, you are making it up.

That very wall is not the wall you see,
not even the one the cyclist wobbled into;
the sun is not what's felt on the freckled arm;
the coathanger is not the noise it makes.

But they're not what's awkward. The brain is un-apt.
The mollusc Nautilus fills its rough eye
with sea-water and never learned to grow
even the mucoid lens of cousin squid
to give it more than a shadow of light.

XX

Into our same kind of cup the light pours
abundantly, is marshalled to needlepoint
and still the brain fumbles grey into black.

And so the lofty real can squire it forever:
unfelt gravities on the sun, sounds a dog
cannot hear, the slight secretive jostle
of particles in the unnameable wall.

Mass, shape, motion how mighty you are!
How centreless, featureless, how bleached
innocent of purpose, how little fussed!
You are the lordly nothing that is. You can
deliver us from ourselves. And that is all.

XXI

– poppy-headed, face down in the pharmacist's drawer –
Bertrand de Born swinging his own head by the hair
like a lantern crying *'Oh me!'* – mind waved aside –

not that being there in that allotment,
surrounded by the neat black soil was strange,
but that suddenly it was strange being anywhere.
So be nowhere – *'with that hair you're the one'll*

stick out, you're not mousey like the rest of them.'
One millet grain of notice blown to you
across the floor should be sufficient.
In the womb neurons die to perfect their brain
then all these bits stipple it as your own. Oh me!

XXII

Old ladies love strange flowers and their Latin names –
even in mid-winter they go to the Alpine
Garden to visit them and shuffle the snow aside.

From the cindered path and tidy soil step back –
'Contemplate Nature in her full grand majesty.'
Scar-y. The infinite and nothing. What
each of us is compared with all that existence.

From the landau of Significance what
can be seen of us, or of neat tabs in felt-tip
tucked in the soil? But if we are nothing
so is the distance from us no more
than the thumb that brushes clear the flower's name.

XXIII

The red-headed pupil is worried he is
not following. Now he's let his mind go
to the sudden sweet crust of a bread-cake.

He tries harder. Tulp quotes Eucalyptus:
*'The search for reality is as momentous
as the search for God.'* And as difficult.
And perhaps the same thing. In there, minus

its life-blood, is the cadaver's mind; in
the cat's cave of his chest his heart; sticking out
his gawky feet – all planetary stuff,
including, even though evaporated now,
'What makes you so different?' 'Me feet, sarge, me feet.'

The Red-Headed Pupil

Part Two: Free Rein

I

Ecce our Jack ski-ing in the Lebanon.
Look at the smile on his face, pleased as Punch,
and just like the Aly Khan in those sunglasses.

He never did it again after the war,
but did smile truly through forty years
an insurance man – ledger, comptometer,
spreadsheet – a fine filament of it all.

The transports dot the screen above Aleppo,
levering south in wireless range of where Cain
slew Abel, and, not knowing what to do
with him, bore him on his back for forty years,
a private lifetime: brother, aircraftman.

II

Ecce the thumps and transactions of Empire:
the trowel-taps of Marduk's bricklayers,
the panel-beaters of Abilene,

the mollusc searched for its purple,
the Druze to market for his Yorkshire worsted,
the Roman miles of water carried as gently
as in a cup so the warm fig will swell,

confectionery saved for Tamburlaine in snow,
the cumulus of all things nice that made
Zenobia Queen of Arabia for a while,
wordperfect Macaulay, the Lady of Battles
with her lionhearts – Ishtar Regina.

III

And the dry-docks of Tyre, and the pepper roads
where styles of diplomacy could be pressed
and Phoenicians write their bills of sale

in letters that would spider this far
so cenotaphs can speak the names they know,
the 10000 souls under their revets of sand,
the dry mold from which the warrior is cast.

To resist Assyria, Ishtar astride her lion,
arrayed in terror, a star in her hair...
...700 chariots...10000 foot...
walking to the railway to the war;
simply put: nude sword to naked abdomen.

IV

To resist Assyria (Ishtar upon her lion)
a democratic vista:
Nell and Perce and Gladys and Jack:

the we the people who are the *matériel*,
the hands between the biscuit and the glaze
colouring cornflowers fifteen to the dozen
or banding Etruscanware for table and sideboard,

and saffruck, the fitters and the clerks,
the servers of school dinners,
the spotters of paths in the sky, dust clouds
in the desert, the dead of the prison-ship,
Nell and Perce and Gladys and Jack.

[after Emyr Humphreys]

V

Suppose, consider, behold, see, know
these four and all those who for any hour
of these fifty thousand years have been a part –

dying in muffled labour for the species,
dreaming of the evening and a game of bowls,
deciding... What is it I ask you find
to do with them, and how, and why?

Only... think... Think of the number, and that
however hurried on their way, none was a speck,
a bit of all there is, of 'what happens',
not the poorest he and she of them but had
and has a life to live. Think of yourself.

VI

Once plumbed in as philosophy, that ancient rage
must now be able to describe not only
what we need but what we expect to be.

The newest child, underwater in a warm pool,
grinning and knowing from its body
how to turn and breathe without a thought,
and the silken light and the fields of morn.

And press on, beyond what it is *like* to be,
to the moment we can truly cry
'This is freedom, here is liberty!
This is what the foot does when the shackle's struck.'
'And down that long dark lode he skated home':

VII

Free of the march for water with an Esso can;
Free of a pop belly and grass rubbed into dust;
Free of prizing a yard of plastic as riches;

Free of gutrot, revenges, falling and sleeping;
Free of him who is exactly stronger,
the boy in judgement killing for beers and Marlboros;
Free of the bridewell and the fortress of angels;

Free of the correct listener and all nuance;
Free of skin, free of hair, of elocution, being tallest;
Free of love received and owed even past death;
Free of all believing, given or sought after;
Free to understand everything, to be beyond and nothing.

VIII

A long draught he took, and again drank deep,
into the rose-girt cistern plunged his face,
bathed in running water, as is the law.

Here on four inches of map from Punjab to the Atlas
are all the palm groves known – for five millennia
all the slow, slow bedding-in of humankind
in towns lost but alive on the 'waterless sea'.

Praise be then to every pipe-layer in his ditch,
to the stolid inspector with his wooden wand,
the Sanitary Idea and all the Chamberlains
and Averys who took the Water Works –
life and death, not source for profit – for their Birminghams.

IX

'Hunger,' said the poet, 'I can bind here
in my own entrails as tight as that most
dextrous of girls can wind a thread.'

Making it something else, does he live on fresh air?
Yet it is said the Prophet himself left this life
without feasting once on barley bread –
white flour and buttered cakes were dreams.

By tightened guts then are we come,
with – the system of account will show –
just enough calorized into the arrowhead
or we would be quite gone into the shale
and our reaching hand never drawn to world attention.

X

I'll eat anything – only cornflakes for a week
when I have to, crisps, custard creams (3p for 2),
grass, starlings, shrews, mice, dog, suck the eyes

from a rat, or an enemy, or those
we did not need, or a hyena itself lined
with carrion, or grains I would not have bruised,
or pekelhareng or pappadelle con sugo pomodori

or blinis or latkes or pagan spice satanic sugar
aubergines in the lake-palace style
the fearsome pineapple bacon and cheese
with oatcakes pikelets black pudding blood
of anything to get by and get by we have.

XI

We've changed it from number 4 to 'Woodford House'.
The wife's done the lettering – she's qualified in that
and always wanted to get back to it.

I did the forecourt to get the van off the avenue
and the hardcore under there's better than the M6 –
you should see their rubbish and weep –
I bevelled the kerb so there's no Council come-back.

Mother would cry if she could see it all.
'Lived in a chimney, us,' she'd say. She gave us
this, framed: *'Who loves not home however poor? /
Himself the master of the door.'* I nearly called this
'The Poorhouse' as a sort of a joke for round here.

XII

It would be. Of all those in the queue that day
who came to breathe in and hold it and go off again,
the shadow stole into the glass for me.

We do not die as much as once we did,
25 per thousand, then 15, and lower,
because of what we got to eat, because
of windows, because of drains and streptomycin.

Into the cold glass as it is slotted to and fro
as I stand hands on hips and hold my breath steals
not *tubercle bacillus* isolated, but a fear
of deserving, a caution set there forever.
What ails me is what I call a shadow.

XIII

From a little German court that could not keep itself
in firewood, to all the Russias of secret prisoners,
imperial house-dogs tried and hanged for treason,

the Empress Catherine rose from snow,
oak-leaves in her hat, a brain in her head
and government felt as a romance, a science,
silver money, no more bits of wood and marten-pelt.

'But the world I found and which we tread,' she said,
'is not an alphabet. Dream it into paradise,
dream it out of all meaning, it was never better
than this, it will never be better than this.
We do not climb the skies, we work on human skin.'

XIV

When I was young and cruel, not Tamburlaine
paddling in human blood, nor yet a true compiler
of human heads as by the road to Nanking,

but pettily, as and when I could, tormenting
the Bible-puncher in the bogs, practising
the reasons why it was all right to do this to him –
all the reasons truly were I could.

So I take my place in the back of the van,
or the gauntlet and don't know what I am,
though if it turns out what I do I'd better not,
or am found out and brought up face to face,
I know I can forget who I ever was.

XV

First off, the hangman couldn't be found no place.
I'd seen him linkin' on out of it
when he saw it comin', but he didn't let on none.

I wished he had though when ole Put turns to me
and says 'Got yourself a new job, Ginge',
and he gets Jones to climb this ladder.
I'm feeling leaky and can't get the necktie fixed.

'Sir,' says Put, 'mend your soul, step off there
and meet your Maker.' Jones don't move a flicker,
just stares out in front. Ole Put gets mad as mad,
skips around and tells me to haul that ladder away.
'No,' I says, 'I ain't goin' to do that.'

XVI

And I dragged the ladder away. When I looked,
Jones's neck was all raw and chicken-stretched,
his legs kicking the last fathom like a clam-diver.

I covered up his face, all black, one eye
clear out on his cheek, and that was so smooth
'cos he'd shaved real careful that morning
as I was standing by him holding the bowl.

And he says to me, 'There ain't no day
not worth shavin' for,' and he winks as he says it.
And I'm glad I remember him as he said that,
and that bowl, 'cos it done me powerful harm
to see what it was I saw that day.

[Homage to S.L. Clemens]

XVII

I am the voice that has been listening all this while,
noted precisely how it is you cannot see
there is no way the subject might be free.

Interrogate, for instance, why you like éclairs.
How was the taste constructed in your mouth?
Was it the lavishment of Mother's 'love',
that old *voyage éclair* the Culture specifies?

The way you wear your hat, especially kiss,
(*monotone et sans éclair*) there are no words
you can control, no blinding *éclairciss-
ement* available to you, I know,
no thundrous no, so – *Vous avez choisi*?

XVIII

That I, a *pícaro*, should fall in love!
And with a slave, a natural slave, a girl
who if she could care would care only for coin.

Nor did I ever take much thought for love,
nor, running low to ground, for honour neither,
not looking for a Helen boasting of gods
on both sides, but never dreaming of a slave,

of finding myself in hiding at the corner,
gawping like a Capuchin when the blacks
celebrate Our Lady of the Snows in dress
barbarous enough to guess their nakedness,
bound to a slave, for her slight limbs shamed.

XIX

The moss-rose and *The Moss-Rose*, red brick
and the redder tree wigged like a dame –
Nell and Perce and Gladys and Jack, father

lifted away. I am in a taxi with the old man
travelling up the hill, the town behind dark,
the road beyond *The Moss-Rose* moorland black,
for a sleeping moment he is back, then gone.

I go to meet my own son by my own route
and am lost in the crescents and walks,
tangled in roadworks-tape, gravel and asphalt piles.
I see him on the walkway, and behind the windscreen
cry, not weep, mouth stretched out and down.

XX

As by Random and Pickle and Clinker, spellbound:
an incident that cooled – out of hot water,
bacteria, mica: lead and flesh – at length a wet

or a dry ape, up from the swamp or down from the trees,
hands for tools, thus mouth for speech (for the not-here,
more later) – for the brain words need: a wide pelvis,
and thus standing is also easy – so onward now,

with culture borne on women's shoulders to make the leaf
grow here and water flow there – a stone roof, a column
and lo, laws and sonnets, and then Steam
who was an Englishman, and Silicon who is not –
like that, like that, like that it was, just like that.

XXI

How beautiful are causes! the sway towards, the click,
the this because of that, the syntax
of predictive power advancing on boiling point.

Yet how we must despise them, hate them
for their fewness, for not demonstrating why
we are unquiet, for being fashioned by us
and so unable just to be themselves.

Yet wish we could descend by them, by degrees,
passing *tubercle bacillus* naked on its slide,
alighting at last in that perfect cold
where every atom stops its shuddering
save the will to know what fact will save her.

XXII

Not that. Not that. Not that. Not that. But I
am still thinking theref... Though I'd rather be –
as who would not? – nicely fat, really comfy

in winceyette, snug as a bug in a rug. And but
for some tremor or other we could be in the coverlets
of shale, the same bits of what is not, of whatever is
hiccupping through its great extinctions,

but without the t-t-t-ting of Telos – spielos Telos,
forget we ever thought of you, out of sight
out of... ah hah! nothing to believe with
and thus free as... stop it!... just free as...
living as though [ ] don't exist. Dream on.

XXIII

In the evening, paddling pools glimpsed from a train;
a yellow squash full of the leaning sun;
a life, a very liveable life, we like more and more.

We all have projects for such happiness:
'For six months I was a French polisher in Newhaven
but all I wanted to do was sing in a band
and the world co-operated and I do.'

'He raped my daughter (12). I picked him up
from prison and took him back. Why did I?
It wasn't me. If you stand back and look at it
you'd see everything's like that, we're pushed,
and what you think is, it doesn't matter, this.

XXIV

'Then again something won't go away –
something, I can't tell what, but it says
I'm not as numb as that tree and don't want to be.'

Pouf! the Empire falls out of mind as she speaks.
Pouf! the boy kisses his captor's face.
Pouf! the old soldier spits out his plug.
'Don't want to be. Don't want to be. Don't want to be.'

A dream is not freedom but it freely comes.
It says: 'Your mind walked up here,
granite and schist underfoot, and is now
what you have become. It invented freedom
as it came, make of it what you can or will.'

The Weak Spot

As if getting by,
doing a job,
roadworks, credit cards
the kid in 3 Windsor
who spits at your back,
watching and loving
your own kids
is not enough –

A swatch of her blood
drops on the tablecloth,
beads and sizzles
on the hotplates
of nan bread and dansak
as she gropes
with a napkin
to mop her nose
split and skee-wiff
– and this in public!
friends around, jumping up,
one crashing across
the table, some of them
in tears,
and it's not something
even the waiters see
too often –
who's going to sort it?
get this guy out?
And what kind of a man
does that?
The heel of his hand
back-handed
though there are
plenty to say
she's mad as an axe
has studied burglary
maybe murder

figuring out ways
to get even
wreck his place
rip up all those books
most of them
the same as she has
Viragos Paladins Vikings
The Condition of the
Working-Class in England
The Interpretation of Dreams
– all so far above
the rock and water universe
the eventual
green universe
past uninformed necessity
even the fresh red
universe of beasts –
and maybe both know
that bit of Freud
where he says about
human cultural development
and sexuality
being still
the weak spot.

Thesaurus:
377 Physical Pleasure
bodily enjoyment
gusto *bonne bouche*
378 Physical Pain
chafe sting bite stab.

*

Who will in
fairest book
of Nature know
how Virtue
may best lodged
in Beauty be,

let him . . .
    the blush of honour
the half-blown
rose

*

blossom from the car-park
tree scratches
the street –
the girls
bared and starved
as needles
greenish in the sodium
light, chlorotic,
stuff such as
a strong wind
would blow away,
first woundable
now maimed,
heroin pushed up
between the toes,
do the work
of beauty,
hanging by the wall
for john,
quids in and
bob or two john,
lickerous john,
his mind greased
to pay
and bruise for it,
peeled from
the starling swarm.

*

(from Charles Baudelaire,
'A celle qui est trop gaie')

Your head, your walk, each move of your mouth
Are like a scene in Nature
Ideally composed, the feature
That is your smile a zephyr from the south.

Any mournful man you brush by in the street
Starts, and, dazzled, steals a glance
Over his shoulder at the dance
Of your shoulder, feels its rush of heat.

When you dress, colour meets colour and halts
Amazed, each shade beating one
Upon another, taffeta silk and chiffon –
You make flowers, the poet says, waltz.

Those crazy clothes show every hue
Of what you are and each fevered part
Sets fire to some patch of my heart –
I hate you as much as adore you!

When I have got myself dressed,
Dragged myself out into the air
Of some bright garden what happens there
But the sun tears at my breast.

Springtime, greenery, the untrodden way,
All the spume of Nature's incense
Shames me to take offence,
To make one flower, one petal pay.

That's you. One night, as desire demands,
I'll come to you, slinking like a coward
Of course to your endowered
Body, and take it in my hands.

That lightsome flesh I'll then chastise,
That blameless breast prise apart,
The rib sprung back above your heart,
The gashes widening before your eyes,

And, in the vertigo of this delicious state,
Across that tender lip –
So beautiful, so sisterly – slip
The fine filtration of perfected hate.

Notes

THE RED-HEADED PUPIL
Part One: The Anatomy Lesson

Rembrandt's *The Anatomy Lesson of Dr Nicholas Tulp*
'shows the master-surgeon surrounded by eager-eyed disciples, in the
act of dissecting the left arm of a corpse. The apparent rendering of a
real moment involved a good deal of artistic licence since dissection,
at that time, started at the stomach, not the arm.'
The Anatomy Lesson of Dr Johan Deyman
'In this, the doctor's assistant holds the top of the skull inverted in his
hand like a small basin while the doctor unravels the cadaver's brain.
It hangs down on either side of the face like an old pullover. The
viewer stares at the underside of the dead man's pale feet.'
Adam Hopkins, *Holland, Its History, Paintings and People*,
Faber & Faber, 1988, pp.69 & 80.

'What is needed is something we do not have: a theory of conscious
organisms as physical systems composed of chemical elements and
occupying space, which also have an individual perspective on the
world, and in some cases the capacity for self-awareness as well.'
Thomas Nagel, *The View from Nowhere*, Oxford University Press,
1986, p.51.

XII   George B. Bridgman, *The Human Machine: The anatomical
structure and mechanism of the human body*, 1938; Dover, New York,
1972.

XIII   'That supples...' Edward Young, citation in *Shorter Oxford
English Dictionary* for *lubricate*.

XV & XVI   'this loam...' Shakespeare, *A Midsummer Night's Dream*,
Act V, Sc i.

XVI   '... the primary visual cortex (also known as the striate cortex or
area 17), the most elementary of the cortical regions concerned with
vision.' *The Brain: A Scientific American Book*, 1979, p.84.

XVIII   'First, Darwin argues that evolution has no purpose.

Individuals struggle to increase the representation of their genes in future generations, and that is all...'
Stephen Jay Gould, *Ever Since Darwin: Reflections in Natural History*, 1978; Pelican Books 1980, p.12.

XIX On 'The mollusc Nautilus...' Richard Dawkins, *The Blind Watchmaker*, 1986; Penguin Books, 1988, pp.85-6.

XXI Bertrand de Born, in Dante, *Inferno*, Canto XXVIII, l 121-3.

XXII 'Let man then contemplate the whole of nature in her full and grand majesty, and turn his vision from the low objects which surround him.'
from Pascal, *Pensée* 72, trans. W.F. Trotter, Everyman, 1931.

XXIII 'Professor Eucalyptus said, "The search
       For reality is as momentous as
       The search for god."'
from Wallace Stevens, 'An Ordinary Evening in New Haven', XXII, *Collected Poems*, Faber & Faber, 1955, p.481.

Part Two: Free Rein

'We cannot help acting under the idea of freedom, it seems; we are *stuck* deliberating as if our futures were open.'
Daniel C. Dennett, *Elbow Room, The Varieties of Free Will Worth Wanting*, Clarendon Press, Oxford, 1984, p.108.

I 'The people say that Cain slew Abel in the village of Zebdany ten miles to the north, and that for forty years he carried him on his back, not knowing what to do with him. On the slopes of this mountain he noticed a raven which was digging a hole to bury one of its kin; so he copied the bird and interred his own brother there.'
Colin Thubron, *Mirror to Damascus*, 1967; Century edition 1986, p.22.

IV 'Tom Williams, Guto, Dick Williams, Wil bach, Dafydd Dew
                                  and me,
       We are the people;'
from Emyr Humphreys, 'A Democratic Vista' XV of *Ancestor Worship*, Gwasg Gee, Denbigh, 1970.

V 'The poorest he that is in England has a life to live as the greatest he, and therefore...every man that is to live under a government ought first by his own consent to put himself under that government.' Colonel Rainborough at the 'Putney Debates', 1647, as quoted in Christopher Hill, *The Century of Revolution, 1603-1714*, Thos Nelson, Edinburgh, 1961, pp.130-1.

VI 'Down that long dark lode...he...skated home'. Charles Kingsley, citation in *Shorter Oxford English Dictionary* for *lode*.

IX 'Immensity and emptiness: poverty and destitution. "I can lock my hunger in the coils of my entrails," writes an Arab poet, "as firmly as a skilful spinning-girl holds in her hand the threads her fingers twist." It was one of the companions of Muhammad, Abu Huraira, who said of the Prophet, "He went out of this world without once feasting on barley bread." Even in the heart of the richest countries, in Baghdad, how many poor men, like the humble folk in the *Thousand and One Nights*, have dreamed of a buttered cake made with white flour!'
Fernand Braudel, *The Mediterranean and the Mediterranean World in the Age of Philip II*, Volume I, 1949, 1966; trans. Sian Reynolds, Fontana/Collins, London, 1975, p.173.

XI 'Who loves not home...' from W.J. Linton, 'Bob Thin, or The Poorhouse Fugitive' (1845), in Brian Maidment, *The Poorhouse Fugitives, Self-taught poets and poetry in Victorian Britain*, Carcanet, Manchester, 1987, p.80.

XXII 'If humans are seen as aspects of a process, they are seen as worked over by such massive mechanisms as natural selection, the process through which survival of traits is determined by the environment. The subjective viewpoints of creatures are of little interest and, in fact, raise the spectre of what evolutionists term the "teleological fallacy" (the fallacy that subjective purposes affect the evolutionary process, which, instead, should be seen as governed by the law of natural selection regardless of any petty motives and purposes of the creatures involved, including humans).'
James L. Peacock, *The Anthropological Lens, Harsh Light, Soft Focus*, Cambridge University Press, 1986, pp.98-9.

XXIII 'We must turn our attention to the circumstances in which people act and by which they are formed, and we must change the

question from "How should we live, whatever the circumstances?" to "Under what circumstances is it possible to live as we should?"'
Thomas Nagel, *Equality and Partiality*, Oxford University Press, 1991, p.52.

*

The Weak Spot
'For the moment perhaps I was Frazer and she was confirming that no matter what complication, injury, foulness, she didn't back down from her belief that all rested on the gentleness in privacy of man and woman – they did in willing desire what in the rock and water universe, the green universe, the bestial universe, was done from ignorant necessity.'
Saul Bellow, *The Adventures of Augie March*, 1953; Penguin edition, 1966, p.317.